COVENANT

By Kenneth E. Hagin

Chapter 1
SATAN'S BIGGEST LIE

*Fools because of their transgression, and
because of their iniquities, are afflicted.*

*Their soul abhorreth all manner of meat; and
they draw near unto the gates of death.*

*Then they cry unto the Lord in their trouble, and
he saveth them out of their distresses.*

*He sent his word, and healed them, and deliv-
ered them from their destructions.*

—Psalm 107:17-20

    I've often made confessions for healing from
the 107th Psalm; particularly from verse 20:
"He sent his word, and healed them. . . ."

2 .

To better understand the meaning of this text, we must look at the entire Psalm. Bear in mind it refers to the children of Israel and the fact that God had provided healing for them.

For example, in Exodus 23 He said, *"And ye shall serve the Lord your God, and he shall bless thy bread and thy water: AND I WILL TAKE SICKNESS AWAY FROM THE MIDST OF THEE. There shall nothing cast their young, nor be barren, in thy land: THE NUMBER OF THY DAYS I WILL FULFIL"* (vv. 25,26).

You can readily see, then, why God calls the children of Israel "fools" in Psalm 107:17. They could have chosen to live in a place in God where there wouldn't have been any sick among them—not in the whole tribe—not in the whole nation.

There was a place in God they could have chosen to live where His blessing would have been on them, their fields, their flocks and herds, and so on. He even promised to fulfill the number of their days, and to bless them above all the peoples on the earth. And what was the blessing? Healing, health, and prosperity.

God established a covenant with them; they

had protection under this Old Covenant. They were foolish to take themselves out from under that kind of a blessing, weren't they?

We've got a covenant, too: the New Covenant. But the way some people preach, I don't think they have ever read the verse in Hebrews that says we have a *better* covenant than the one the children of Israel had:

HEBREWS 8:6
6 But now hath he obtained a more excellent ministry, by how much also he is the mediator of A BETTER COVENANT, which was established upon BETTER PROMISES.

(I think if they read it at all, they thought it said "worse"!)

All of our lives we've heard in church that God doesn't want us to have anything. We're to go through life on Barely-Get-Along Street, 'way down at the end of the block, next to Grumble Alley, and never have anything. We're to be sick, afflicted, and down-trodden all our lives, and *maybe* we can *barely* get into Heaven.

No wonder that turns a lot of people off! Is a

covenant with *no* healing and *no* prosperity a true picture of this *better* covenant? You don't get that kind of picture under the *Old* Covenant, yet this New Covenant is supposed to be a *better* covenant.

Would Jesus the Son of God have come to be a mediator between God and man for a covenant that is not so good as the Old Covenant? How foolish! Yet the Church as a whole has been hoodwinked by the devil. I think the devil slipped that over on the Church, because he knew if the Church prospered, Christians would send the message of salvation around the world. But if he could slip up on their blind side and make them believe they shouldn't have any of "this world's goods," they wouldn't prosper and therefore wouldn't evangelize.

God wants to bless His people! Although the world system *is* wrong, the world's goods *aren't* wrong. In fact, they are not really the goods of this world system. Who made these things? God did. He made the silver, the gold, and the cattle on a thousand hills. *"The earth is the Lord's, and the fulness thereof,"* the Bible says (Ps. 24:1).

God made it and gave it all to Adam. But Adam committed high treason and turned it over to Satan. It's certain Satan doesn't want you to get it back, so he lies to Christians and they swallow his lie. They think they are being humble by not wanting any of "this world's goods." Bless their hearts, they don't know they are being stupid.

They agree it's all right for the devil and his crowd to have this world's goods, but not the Church. They agree that Church members ought to go through life with their noses to the grindstone, barely making it.

Was God that kind of God under the Old Covenant? No.

Well, what made Him change? He didn't change. He couldn't change. The Bible says (James 1:17) there is not even a "shadow of turning" with Him.

Glory to God, He is not a God of poverty; He is a God of plenty!

Why should the people of God be a people of poverty? They shouldn't. That kind of teaching has filtered into our minds until it has been difficult for us to accept the truth. But if your heart's in tune with God, it repels that teaching.

Chapter 2
WHY CHRISTIANS ARE SICK

"Fools because of their transgression, and because of their iniquities, are afflicted." I know God is talking about the Jews here, but this also could apply to us.

Most Christians are sick because they do not know their rights and privileges in Christ. They don't know what belongs to them. And once they begin to understand a little about what does belong to them, they don't know how to take advantage of it. Still others know the truth, but have willfully taken themselves out from under the protection of the New Covenant.

We need to study these covenants. We need to know for ourselves what our rights and privileges are under them, and we need to share this knowledge with other people. Some will rise to the level of this teaching and will enjoy walking in the light of it.

It was because of Israel's *persistence* in doing wrong that they were afflicted. As we saw, they didn't *have* to be sick unto death. God gave them the Old Covenant. He showed them what to do.

Thank God for His mercy. Does the Bible say, "Then they cry unto the Lord in their trouble and He says, 'Goody, goody. I told you you were going to get it! That's good enough for you, you reprobate bunch of backslidden buzzards. I told you what was going to happen to you, and you wouldn't listen'"?

No, that's not what He said. That's not the picture the Bible gives me of my Father. Aren't you glad? (He may be God to the world, but He's Father to me.)

The Bible says, *"He saveth them out of their distresses. He sent his word, and HEALED them, and delivered them from their destructions"* (vv. 19,20).

The next verse begins: *"Oh that men would praise the Lord for his GOODNESS...."* (v. 21). What was just discussed in connection with the goodness of the Lord? Healing. (*"He sent his word, and healed them."*)

"Oh that men would praise the Lord for his goodness, and for his wonderful works to the children of men." That sounds like Acts 10:38, a New Testament Scripture we often have referred to: *"How God* [this same God] *anointed*

Jesus of Nazareth with the Holy Ghost and power, who went about DOING GOOD AND HEALING ALL that were oppressed of the devil."

Notice that *doing good* and *goodness* are mentioned in the Bible in connection with *healing*.

In the past, we have limited the goodness of God to His goodness to forgive sins. Thank God for it, but if that's all you emphasize, that's all people will believe for.

Think about God's goodness: He hasn't changed; He's just as good as He ever was.

God is a good God. Shut your eyes and say it out loud: "God is a good God."

Oral Roberts has emphasized this. I've been present when he's preached it, and I've heard Full Gospel preachers say, "Yeah, but you've got to remember. . . ." I've thought to myself, *What else would you say? "God is a BAD God"? or "God is a MEAN God"?* Yet that's the impression the preachers left. If God is not good, what kind of God is He?

God is a good God. I believe He's totally good—100 percent good. Furthermore, healing is good. I know: I was physically incapacitated for the first 16 years of my life because of my deformed heart.

Then I became bedfast 16 long months, flat on my back. At times I was totally paralyzed. They had to turn me on a sheet. Somebody had to feed me. I had an incurable blood disease which would have killed me if the deformed heart didn't. Then God healed me.

So I've been sick and I've been well, and well is better. God wants *you* well, too.

Say it out loud: "God wants me well."

If sick people would just say that over and over again—2,000 or 10,000 times—it would finally dawn on their spirits, and they would get in line with what God wants.

If you listen to some people, though, they'll say that God wants you sick! I hardly dare say it, but let's just *pretend* God wants me to be sick. . . . Oh my, something right down inside of me starts rebelling against that when I even *think* it!

You see, *your spirit knows more than your head does*. Once you have been born again, your spirit—your innermost being—has the life and nature of God in it.

Let me ask you this: If God wants you sick, why do you want to get well? Why go to the hospital for an operation if God wants you sick? You'd be out of the will of God. Why take even an aspirin if God wants you sick? Why don't you just keep your headache if it's God's will for you?

Doctors believe God wants us well; otherwise, they'd be working against God. God wants you well. God wants me well.

Chapter 3
WONDERFUL WORKS

"Oh that men would praise the Lord for his goodness, and for his wonderful works to the children of men." And these "wonderful works" are connected with healing:

JOHN 14:10-12
10 Believest thou not that I am in the Father, and the Father in me? the words that I speak unto you I speak not of myself: but the Father that dwelleth in me, he doeth the WORKS.
11 Believe me that I am in the Father, and the Father in me: or else believe me for the very WORKS' sake.
12 Verily, verily, I say unto you, He that believeth on me, the works that I do shall he do also; and GREATER WORKS than these shall he do; because I go unto my Father.

In these three verses, Jesus is talking about works. Keep "works" in mind and go back again to Psalm 107, verses 20 and 21: *"He sent his word, and healed them, and delivered them from their destructions. Oh that men would praise the Lord for his goodness, and for HIS*

WONDERFUL WORKS to the children of men."

Have part of His wonderful works been done away with? Are His works limited to salvation? No, thank God. These "wonderful works" are mentioned in connection with healing.

That's what Jesus was talking about in John 14, when He said, *"He that believeth on me, the WORKS that I do. . . ."* What works did Jesus do? He went about *"doing good and healing all"* who were oppressed of the devil.

If you carefully read through the four Gospels, you will find Jesus spent 75 percent of His time ministering to the sick—healing the sick.

Even Pentecostal preachers have said to me, "Well, you know, healing was just a side issue with Jesus and the disciples." I never let them bother me the least. I kept ministering to the sick. Healing is not a sideline; it's the main line. God is not off on a sideline. His goodness and wonderful works are the same. He is the same God now He was then.

PSALM 107:22
22 And let them sacrifice the sacrifices of

14

thanksgiving, and declare his works with rejoicing.

What "works" is the Psalmist talking about? The works mentioned in the previous verse: *"He sent his word, and healed them, and delivered them from their destructions."*

It's quite obvious that the reason for sickness and disease among the children of Israel was because they had rebelled against the Word of God. They had condemned the counsel of the Most High (v. 11). They had taken themselves out from under the protection of the Old Covenant. *"Fools because of their transgression, and because of their iniquities, are afflicted."*

Was it God's will for them to be afflicted? No, it wasn't. He's the same God now He was then. I don't believe He has changed one iota. I believe He's just as full of goodness now as He was then. I believe He's doing the same works now that He did then.

I know it from experience (this is what separates the men from the boys). I've been preaching for more than 45 years. I believe that *it's the plan of God the Father that no believer should ever be sick.* I believe that's His plan. It's not fully carried out, because people don't know what His plan is. They don't know how to cooperate with Him.

Once you start preaching the plan of the Father on this subject, nearly everybody is ready to attack you! Wonderful people—saved, filled with the Holy Spirit, people who speak with other tongues, good friends. "Oh," they say, "now he's getting too far out!"

Well, do you mean God planned that we be sick? Did He plan that Israel be sick? It seems to me as I read this passage of Scripture that His plan was that they shouldn't be sick. I know they were sick, but that wasn't His plan for them.

After all, Israel were not the sons of God; they were the *servants* of God. But under this better covenant, established on better promises, we've become *sons* of God!

1 JOHN 3:2
2 Beloved, now are we the SONS of God, and it doth not yet appear what we shall be: but we know that, when he shall appear, we shall be like him; for we shall see him as he is.

If it wasn't His plan for His *servants* to be sick, why would it be His plan for his *sons* to be sick?

His plan for His servants was: *"I will take sickness away from the midst of thee... The number of thy days I will fulfil...."* If that's His plan for His *servants,* could His plan for His *sons* be any less? Would He love His sons less than He loves His servants?

No, thank God—a thousand times no! *I believe it is the plan of the Father that no believer should ever be sick; he should live his full length of time on this earth and actually wear out and fall asleep.*

Furthermore, *I believe it is not my Father's will that we should suffer with cancer and other dread diseases* that bring such pain and anguish.

Of course, if you preach these things, you'll get criticized. They'll even accuse you of being a cult. Isn't that something? Called a cult for believing the Bible! Even Pentecostals will say this. Well, they can believe what they want to; I'll just believe the Bible.

Some will argue, "God uses sickness and

disease to teach us."

Did He use sickness and disease to teach Israel? No, He gave them His Word and said, "Walk in it and you won't be sick. I'll take sickness away from the midst of you. I'll bless you above all peoples everywhere, and the number of your days you'll fulfill."

If you go back to the 28th chapter of Deuteronomy, you will see that God told them what the blessings would be if they kept His commandments, and what the curses would be if they failed to keep His commandments.

But His way of teaching them wasn't putting sickness and disease on them. That's human reasoning; that's the peanut brain of theologians trying to deal with a biblical truth by interpreting it in the light of what they see.

They see a good man, a preacher of the Gospel, get cancer. He suffers, and suffers, and suffers, and finally dies. Well, I regret that as much as they do, but I still don't believe that's the plan of the Father God or His way to teach that preacher something.

The children of Israel became sick because of broken laws—because of sinning against the

Word of God. Although I'm speaking about the Jews, the same principle can apply to us today.

Bear in mind that as long as the children of Israel kept the covenant law, no illness was among them, but when they sinned, their bodies became filled with diseases. Even then, however, they had a right to turn to the Lord and find forgiveness and healing.

Well, we have a better covenant established on better promises. If we keep our covenant, will the same principles work for us that worked under the Old Covenant? I believe so.

Chapter 4
THE LAW OF LOVE

A new commandment I give unto you, That ye love one another; as I have loved you, that ye also love one another.

—John 13:34

What is this "new" commandment? The Old Covenant had the Ten Commandments, but we don't have to bother about commandments under the New.

When we say this, people immediately ask, "You mean we don't have to keep the Ten Commandments?"

Wait a minute. Notice this: *"A NEW COMMANDMENT I give unto you, that YE LOVE one another. . . ."*

If you walk in love, you're not going to break any of the commandments that were given to curb sin. A commandment doesn't have to be written for you stating, "Thou shalt not steal from your neighbor." If you love him, you're not going to steal from him.

But how are you going to love with that God-kind of love? *God furnishes it!* Isn't that wonderful? No wonder this is a better covenant. God furnishes His love to us, enabling us to keep the covenant. The Bible says, *"The love of God is shed abroad in our hearts by the Holy Ghost"* (Rom. 5:5).

If you have been born again, the love of God is there in your heart (spirit). Let His love dominate you.

Several years ago, while my wife and I were preaching in a western state, we met a young couple whose 3-year-old daughter had epilepsy.

They took her to the leading specialist West of the Mississippi River. After running a brain scan and other tests, he said hers was the worst case he'd seen in 40 years of practicing medicine.

The parents were trying to believe God for the child's healing. When we first met them, we counseled the mother about a problem she had been having with relatives.

One day they called the motel where we were staying. I was getting ready to go to church—I was shaving, actually—and I heard

my wife say, "Well, he doesn't ever go unless the
Lord tells him." You get so many calls you
couldn't answer every request; that's all you'd
be doing. If the Lord says, "Go" (which He sel-
dom does), I go. If He doesn't, I don't.

This time the Spirit of God said, "Go," so I
stuck my head out of the bathroom door and
said, "Who is it?" She told me, and I said, "Tell
them we'll be there in about 10 minutes."

I assumed the Lord wanted me to go pray for
the little girl, but as I finished dressing, the
Spirit of God spoke to my spirit, saying, "Don't
pray for the child. Don't lay your hand on her.
Don't anoint her with oil.

"Say to the mother, 'I said to Israel, "Walk in
my statutes and keep my commandments, and
I'll permit none of these diseases upon thee
which I permitted upon the Egyptians, for I am
the Lord that healeth thee. I'll take sickness
away from the midst of thee, and the number of
thy days I will fulfil."

" 'You keep my commandment of love, walk
in my statute of love, and I'll take sickness
away from the midst of thee, and the number of
your days you'll fulfill. Say to Satan, 'Satan, I'm

walking in love. Now you take your hand off my child!' "

I told her what the Lord said. She took hold of it like a dog does a bone, and ran off with it. I mean, I hadn't gotten it out of my mouth until she stomped her foot and boldly said, "Satan, I'm walking in love. You take your hand off my child!"

Do you know what happened? As fast as you could snap your finger, the child's epileptic seizures stopped.

Somebody will ask, "What if she hadn't done that?"

Her child would still have epilepsy.

I'm well convinced that there is a truth here that's been hidden from the church.

Folks need to see in their spirits, not just in their heads, that our covenant is better and if we do what He said and walk in His commandment of love, He will take sickness away from the midst of us and fulfill the number of our days.

I know from experience—I've been preaching more than 45 years—that if you're going to walk in divine health, you're going to have to walk in love. You can't hold a grudge and get rid of sickness. If you've got animosity toward someone, confess it. God will *forgive* your iniquities and *heal* your diseases.

Years ago I purposed in my heart to walk in love toward my fellow man—my fellow minister, whomever—regardless of what they did or said. I'm going to walk in love whether anybody else does or not!

Oh, I've been tempted—my, my, I've been tempted. All of us will be tempted. It's not a sin to be tempted; it's a sin to yield to temptation.

We had almost constant revival in one church I pastored. God was blessing us so greatly that the place was packed every Sunday night. In warm weather, there would be as many standing outside looking in as there were inside. We had days of heaven on earth—a constant manifestation of the move of the Spirit of God.

Well, I eventually went on somewhere else and another fellow took the church. Later, when I was pastoring down in East Texas, my father-in-law asked me what had happened to my former pastorate. "We went down there

Sunday night," he said, "and there were 40 people out. The building was virtually empty."

I went to see this new pastor. I knew, because of what he had said to somebody else, that he was blaming me for his failure. Well, that's human nature—and that human nature came from the devil.

The first thing Adam did when God asked, "Adam, where art thou?" was to say, "I hid myself." And when God asked him why, Adam replied, *"The woman whom thou gavest to be with me, she gave me of the tree, and I did eat."* He started blaming it on God and the woman! "The woman. . .the woman. . .the woman *thou* gavest me. . . . You did it. You did it, God. You're the One who did it." That's human nature: blaming it on someone else.

I knew this preacher had said something to other preachers; that's one of the reasons I went by the parsonage to see him. I asked, "How are things going?"

"Well," he said, "they couldn't be worse." He went on to tell me about it.

I said, "One thing about it—I want you to know I haven't gotten any money from any of the folks in this church—none of your tithes, none of your money or anything.

Oh, he just blew up! "I know better! You've been coming around visiting my members," he said. (And I hadn't visited any of them.)

I was sitting in the car, and he was standing outside. The window was down. He reached in, got hold of my tie, and started choking me. Right under that car seat I had a tire tool. I reached down, got hold of it, and came very near to knocking the fellow in the head with it. Oh, the flesh wanted to so bad!

If I had yielded to the flesh, wouldn't that have made a good headline in the newspaper: "Two Full Gospel Preachers in a Fight"?

But I refused to yield to the flesh. I had determined to let the love of God dominate me. So I turned loose of that tire tool.

I let the love that's in me just bubble up. I said to him, "Dear brother, dear brother . . . ." With tears I said it. With kindness in my voice I said it.

"Dear brother, God is my eternal witness, I know some of the things you are going through. God is my witness, many has been the night at

2, 3 and 4 o'clock in the morning when I've been on my knees on a cold floor in the wintertime praying for you. God is my eternal witness."

As I was saying this, that preacher jumped like I had hit him with a whip every time I opened my mouth. Then he started crying—just boo-hooing. You never saw such tears.

"My God, Brother Hagin," he said, "I want you to forgive me. I got in the flesh. I know you didn't take money from my members. I falsely accused you. I know I did. I guess some of the other brethren told you. I did it, and I knew better."

With tears he said, "I just failed. That's what I did. I didn't have enough sense to know how to handle the situation here, and I wouldn't listen to you." (He had asked me for some advice, and I had given it to him, but he wouldn't listen.)

He said, "I wouldn't listen. I messed the whole thing up. Nobody is to blame but me. I was just looking for a way out." He fell down crying. He said, "Just pray for me and forgive me!"

I said, "I do, praise God. I forgive you."

I believe love is the best way. I know you must walk in love in order to walk in health. I believe there is a real secret here of healing and health.

Chapter 5
THE PROMISE OF LONG LIFE

God is saying to all of us, "Walk in my statute of love, walk in my commandment of love, and I'll take sickness away from the midst of thee, and the number of thy days I will fulfill."

I don't mean by that that you should become passive and do nothing. No, be like the mother of that epileptic child. When Satan's attack comes, take your stand and say, "Satan, I'm walking in love. You take your hands off of me, my family (or whatever else it is you have a right to act for). I'm walking in love."

But because many Christians have not known to do that, they have not taken this stand, and the devil has taken advantage of them.

The same thing happened to the children of Israel under the Old Covenant. You will remember God said on one occasion, *"My people [not the devil's crowd] are destroyed for lack of knowledge"* (Hosea 4:6). The devil took advantage of them, too, because of what they didn't know.

I do not want to leave the impression, however, that the majority of Christians are sick because they have sinned.

I think the majority of Christians are sick because of two reasons: First, they do not know what belongs to them under the covenant; and, second, if they begin to get a little inkling of it, they don't know how to take advantage of it and walk in the light of the New Covenant. Thus, Satan takes advantage of Christians and destroys some of us.

Forget about those wrongs somebody did to you. If you let bitterness fester in your spirit and soul, it will rob you.

I let people say what they want to say about me. I'm not going to take time to deny it; I'm just going to keep shouting the victory. I'm going to maintain a good conscience between myself and God. Those people can't keep me out of Heaven, anyway.

One time my wife and I were holding a meeting in a Full Gospel church, and the pastor asked for a few folks who had gotten something out of the meeting to get up and testify. One lady got up and told about being healed.

Another lady sitting close to my wife said to a friend, "I don't know what *she's* testifying about. She's not even saved!"

Her friend said, "What do you mean she's not saved? Why she's saved, filled with the Holy Ghost, and a member of this church."

"Yes, but she did me wrong. I haven't forgiven her—and besides, I'm not going to! And if I *don't* forgive her, she can't go to heaven!"

(That is ignorance gone to seed. The woman who refused to forgive is the one who isn't going to heaven.)

When we inquired later, we discovered that the woman was angry because she thought this other woman had taken her boyfriend away from her. Actually, he had quit going with her two months before he met the other woman. But the first woman still had it in for her because she got him and married him.

People have all kinds of ideas. A lot of those ideas are keeping them from getting healed—and a lot of those ideas are the reason for their being sick in the first place.

That's the reason they need to get back to

the law of love. The law of love doesn't consider me; it considers the other person. The law of love even works from a natural standpoint.

Several years ago I read an interview a *Time* magazine reporter had with the president of the American Medical Association. The AMA president said, "We've gone in for the specialist and we've left off the old family physician. We run people through our offices just like a number, not like an individual. The old family doctor was closer to people. He knew a lot of things about them.

"Actually, we've lost from the medical profession the greatest healing agency there is: love."

Think about that.

Do you know what God is saying to us? "By this shall all men know that you are my disciples, because you have love one for another. Love one another, even as I have loved you. Walk in my statute of love, keep my commandment of love, and I'll take sickness away from the midst of you. The number of your days I'll fulfill."

How many days is that? Well, in Psalm 91,

the Lord said, *"With long life will I satisfy him."*
So no matter how old you are, if you're not
satisfied yet, keep on living!

Somebody will say, "Well, He just promised
us 70 years."

If you read that again, you'll see that's not a
promise. The Psalmist is lamenting the fact
that *"the days of our years are 70 and by reason
of strength they be fourscore [80] and they are
soon cut off and we fly away."*

So don't stop at less than 70. If you are
satisfied with 70, go on home. If you're not
satisfied, go on up to 80. When you get there, if
you're not satisfied, go on up to 90. If you get
satisfied, then go on home.

Some people, bless their hearts, will say,
"Well, that's far-fetched." But it's Bible principles. Can't you see it?

*"I will take sickness away from the midst of
thee,"* God said, *"the number of thy days I will
fulfil."*

How many is the number of thy days? Until
you get satisfied.